UNTANGLING
FAITH
LEADER GUIDE

UNTANGLING FAITH

Reclaiming Hope in the Questions Jesus Asked

AMBERLY NEESE

Abingdon Women

Nashville

Untangling Faith
Reclaiming Hope in the Questions Jesus Asked
Leader Guide

ISBN 978-1-7910-2876-3

MANUFACTURED IN THE UNITED STATES OF AMERICA

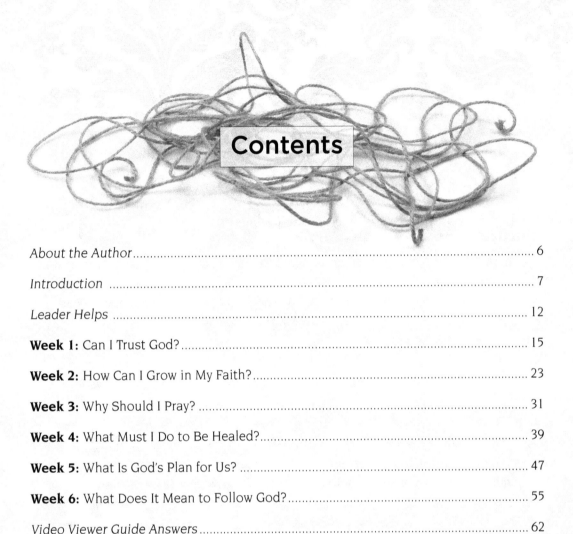

Contents

Amberly Neese is a speaker, humorist, and encourager with a passion for "GRIN-spiring" others. As a featured speaker for the Aspire Women's Events and the main host/comedienne for Marriage Date Night, two popular Christian events that tour nationally, she enjoys touching the hearts and minds and funny bones of people all over the country. The Bible says that laughter is good medicine, and she has found it's also like glue—helping the truths of God's Word to "stick." Amberly loves to remind women of the power and hope found in Scripture. Through a flair for storytelling and a love for Jesus, she candidly opens up her story alongside God's Word to encourage others in their walk with Him.

With a master's degree from Biola University, Amberly serves as an adjunct professor at Grand Canyon University and the Master Connector for Inspiring Growth, an organization developed to equip and encourage growth in leaders and businesses. She is the author of *The Belonging Project: Finding Your Tribe and Learning to Thrive*, *Common Ground: Loving Others Despite Our Differences*, and *The Friendship Initiative: 31 Days of Loving and Connecting Like Jesus*. She and her husband, Scott, have two adult children and live in Prescott, Arizona, where they enjoy the great outdoors, the Food Network, and all things *Star Wars*.

Follow Amberly:

 @amberlyneese

@amberlyneese

@Amberly Neese - Comedian and Speaker

Website: www.amberlyneese.com

Tour information can also be found at marriagedatenight.com and aspirewomensevents.com.

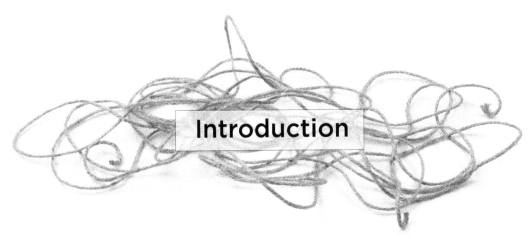

Introduction

Welcome to the *Untangling Faith Leader Guide*. What a wonderful opportunity you have to guide women on a journey of untangling some common faith questions that sometimes tie us up in knots of confusion, discouragement, and disillusionment. Rather than providing answers, your role is to create a safe space for exploring the questions together and, in the process, discovering a more intimate relationship with God.

Regardless of where we are on our faith journey, we all have questions, and the good news is that our questions can actually help us untangle our faith. Jesus loves questions! In the Gospels, he asks over three hundred questions and directly answers only three. By asking so many questions, Jesus invites us to ask, seek, and grapple with our own questions. He knows that our questions can be holy guides leading us to truth and deeper connection with God.

Jesus wants us to know Him in authentic relationship, and a good way to do that is to explore our questions with Him through the lens of the questions He asked while on earth. So, together we will explore six common questions we ask, unpacking one each week through the context of specific questions Jesus asked. These six overarching questions will invite us to view all our questions as sacred tools of connection and discovery:

1. Can I trust God?
2. How can I grow in my faith?
3. Why should I pray?
4. What must I do to be healed?
5. What is God's plan for us?
6. What does it mean to follow God?

About the Participant Book

Before the first session, you will want to distribute copies of the participant workbook to the members of your group. Ideally, you should complete the first week of readings before

your first group session (each video complements the content you explored during the week), but feel free to adapt the format and material as you see fit to best meet the needs of your group. For each week there is a scripture memory verse and five readings or lessons that combine exploration of the questions of Jesus and other scriptures with personal reflection and application. On average, each lesson can be completed in about twenty to thirty minutes. Completing these readings each week will prepare the women for the discussion and activities of the group session.

About This Leader Guide

As you gather each week with the members of your group, you will have the opportunity to watch a video, discuss and respond to what you're learning, and pray together. You will need access to a television and a DVD player with working remotes. Or you may access the videos for this study and other Abingdon Women's Bible studies on AmplifyMedia.com through an individual or church membership.

Creating a warm and inviting atmosphere will help make the women feel welcome. Although optional, you might consider providing snacks and drinks or coffee for your first meeting and inviting group members to rotate in bringing refreshments each week.

This leader guide and the video lessons will be your primary tools for leading each group session. In this book you will find outlines for six group sessions, each formatted for either a 60-minute or 90-minute group session:

60-Minute Format

Leader Prep	(Before the Session)
Welcome and Opening Prayer	5 minutes
Icebreaker	5 minutes
Video	20 minutes
Group Discussion	25 minutes
Closing Prayer	5 minutes

90-Minute Format

Leader Prep	(Before the Session)
Welcome and Opening Prayer	5–10 minutes
Icebreaker	5 minutes
Video	20 minutes

Group Discussion	35 minutes
Deeper Conversation	15 minutes
Closing Prayer	5 minutes

As you can see, the 90-minute format is identical to the 60-minute format but allows more time for the welcome/opening prayer and group discussion plus a Deeper Conversation exercise for small groups. Feel free to adapt or modify either of these formats, as well as the individual segments and activities, in any way to meet the specific needs and preferences of your group.

Here is a brief overview of the elements included in both formats:

Leader Prep (Before the Session)

For your preparation prior to the group session, this section provides an Overview of the week's biblical theme, and a list of materials and equipment needed. Be sure to review this section, as well as read through the *entire* session outline, before your group time in order to plan and prepare. If you choose, you also may find it helpful to watch the video lesson in advance.

Welcome and Opening Prayer (5–10 minutes, depending on session length)

Create a warm, welcoming environment as the women are gathering before the session begins. Consider either lighting one or more candles, providing coffee or other refreshments, or playing worship music, or all of these. (Bring an iPod, smartphone, or tablet and a portable speaker if desired.) Be sure to provide name tags if the women do not know one another or you have new participants in your group. Then, when you are ready to begin, open the group in prayer before you begin your time.

Icebreaker (5 minutes)

Use the icebreaker to briefly engage the women in the topic while helping them feel comfortable with one another.

Video (20 minutes)

Next, watch the week's video segment together. Be sure to direct participants to the Video Viewer Guide in the participant workbook, which they may complete as they watch the video. (Answers are provided on page 62 of this guide and page 218 in the participant workbook.)

Group Discussion (25–35 minutes, depending on session length)

After watching the video, choose from the questions provided to facilitate group discussion (questions are provided for both the video segment and the participant workbook material). For the participant workbook portion, you may choose to read aloud the discussion points or express them in your own words; then use one or more of the questions that follow to guide your conversation.

Note that more material is provided than you will have time to include. Before the session, select what questions you want to ask, putting a check mark beside them in your book. Reflect on each question and make some notes in the margins to share during your discussion time. Page references are provided for those questions that relate to specific questions or activities in the participant workbook. For these questions, invite group members to turn in their books to the pages indicated. Participants will need Bibles in order to look up various supplementary scriptures.

Depending on the number of women in your group and the level of their participation, you may not have time to cover everything you have selected, and that is OK. Rather than attempting to bulldoze through, follow the Spirit's lead and be open to where the Spirit takes the conversation. Remember that your role is not to have all the answers but to encourage discussion and sharing.

Deeper Conversation (15 minutes)

If your group is meeting for 90 minutes, use this exercise for deeper sharing in small groups, dividing into groups of two or three. This is a time for women to share more intimately and build connections with one another. (Encourage the women to break into different groups each week.) Give a two-minute warning before time is up so that the groups may wrap up their discussion.

Closing Prayer (5 minutes)

Close by leading the group in prayer. If you'd like, invite the women to briefly name prayer requests. To get things started, you might share a personal request of your own. As women share their requests, model for the group by writing each request in your participant workbook, indicating that you will remember to pray for them during the week.

As the study progresses, you might encourage members to participate in the Closing Prayer by praying out loud for one another and the requests given. Ask the women to

volunteer to pray for specific requests, or have each woman pray for the woman on her right or left. Make sure name tags are visible so that group members do not feel awkward if they do not remember someone's name.

Before You Begin

Though the circumstances of the women in your group are different, you will find the questions they ask when life is difficult, disappointing, or devastating to be amazingly similar. Even so, the thoughts and feelings they have related to those questions may differ significantly. Encourage the women to listen attentively to one another with gentleness and compassion, refraining from giving advice, minimizing, offering religious platitudes, interrupting to share their own story, or making comments such as "I know exactly how you feel." When someone is sharing vulnerably, one of the greatest gifts we can offer is simply our loving, attentive presence. This allows space for others to hear the "gentle whisper" of God (1 Kings 19:12).

My prayer for you and your group is that this study will remind you that even when your faith feels tangled, God loves you, desires you to seek Him, and welcomes your questions. Jesus promises us, "Ask and it will be given to you; seek and you will find; knock and the door will be opened to you" (Matthew 7:7). I am grateful you have said yes to facilitating this journey of questioning and reclaiming our hope as we grow in our knowledge of the goodness and love of God.

Praying for you,

Amberly

Leader Helps

Preparing for the Sessions

- Decide whether you will use the 60-minute or 90-minute format. Be sure to communicate dates and times to participants in advance.
- If you are following the suggested format, ensure that participants receive their workbooks at least one week before your first session and instruct them to complete the first week's readings. If you have the phone numbers or email addresses of your group members, send out a reminder and a welcome.
- Check out your meeting space before each group session (or set up a virtual meeting and share the link). Make sure the room is ready. Do you have enough chairs? Do you have the equipment and supplies you need? (See the list of materials needed in each session outline.)
- Pray for your group and each group member by name. Ask God to work in the life of every woman in your group.
- Read and complete the week's readings in the participant workbook and review the session outline in the leader guide. Select the discussion points and questions you want to cover and make some notes in the margins to share in your discussion time.

Leading the Sessions

- Personally welcome and greet each woman as she arrives (whether in person or online). You might want to have a sign-up list for the women to record their names and contact information.
- At the start of each session, ask the women to turn off or silence their cell phones (or eliminate other distractions if meeting online).
- Always start on time. Honor the time of those who are punctual.
- Encourage everyone to participate fully, but don't put anyone on the spot. Be prepared to offer a personal example or answer if no one else responds at first.

- Communicate the importance of completing the weekly readings and participating in group discussion.
- Facilitate but don't dominate. Remember that if you talk most of the time, group members may tend to listen rather than to engage. Your task is to encourage conversation and keep the discussion moving.
- If someone monopolizes the conversation, kindly thank her for sharing and ask if anyone else has any insights.
- Encourage participants not to minimize, give advice, offer platitudes, interrupt, or make comments such as "I know exactly how you feel" when another group member is sharing. Remind them that one of the greatest gifts we can offer is our loving, attentive presence, and model this yourself.
- Remind the women that what is shared in the group stays in the group. Confidentiality is essential for creating a safe environment.
- Remember that you are not expected to be the expert or have all the answers. Acknowledge that all of you are on this journey together, with the Holy Spirit as your leader and guide. If issues or questions arise that you don't feel equipped to handle or address, talk with the pastor or a staff member at your church.
- Don't rush to fill the silence. If no one speaks right away, it's OK to wait for someone to answer. After a moment, ask, "Would anyone be willing to share?" If no one responds, try asking the question again a different way—or offer a brief response and ask if anyone has anything to add.
- Encourage good discussion, but don't be timid about calling time on a particular question and moving ahead. Part of your responsibility is to keep the group on track. If you decide to spend extra time on a given question or activity, consider skipping or spending less time on another question or activity in order to stay on schedule.
- End on time. If you are running over, give members the opportunity to leave if they need to. Then wrap up as quickly as you can.
- Thank the women for coming and let them know you're looking forward to seeing them next time.
- Be prepared for some women to want to hang out and talk at the end. If you need everyone to leave by a certain time, communicate this at the beginning of the group session. If you are meeting in a church during regularly scheduled activities, be aware of nursery closing times.

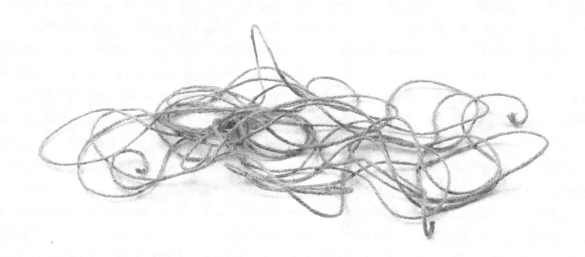

Week 1

Can I Trust God?

Leader Notes for the Week

_____

_____

_____

_____

_____

_____

_____

_____

_____

_____

Week 1 Can I Trust God?

Leader Prep (Before the Session)

Overview

This week we looked closely at the word *trust* and, specifically, our trust in God. We considered questions regarding God's trustworthiness as we explored the nature of God through these five characteristics:

Day 1: God Is a Loving Parent
Day 2: God Is Good
Day 3: God Is Faithful
Day 4: God Is My Safe Place
Day 5: God Desires to Help Us See Clearly

Memory Verse

The LORD is my strength and my shield;
    my heart trusts in him, and he helps me.
My heart leaps for joy,
    and with my song I praise him.
                    (Psalm 28:7)

Daily Questions

Day 1

Jesus's Question: "Which father among you would give a snake to your child if the child asked for a fish?" (Luke 11:11)
The Question We Ask: Does God care about me and my struggle?

Day 2

Jesus's Question: "You of little faith, why are you talking among yourselves about having no bread? Do you still not understand?" (Matthew 16:8-9a)

The Question We Ask: Is everything going to be OK?

Day 3

Jesus's Question: "Can any one of you by worrying add a single hour to your life?" (Matthew 6:27)

The Question We Ask: What's going to happen?

Day 4

Jesus's Question: "Don't you know me...?" (John 14:9)

The Question We Ask: Will God keep me safe?

Day 5

Jesus's Question: "Do you see anything?" (Mark 8:23)

The Question We Ask: Will God complete the work He has begun in me?

What You Will Need

- *Untangling Faith* DVD and DVD player, or equipment to stream the video online
- Bible and *Untangling Faith* participant workbook for reference
- markerboard or chart paper and markers (optional)
- stick-on name tags and markers (optional)
- iPod, smartphone, or tablet and portable speaker (optional)

Session Outline

Welcome and Opening Prayer (5–10 minutes, depending on session length)

In order to create a warm, welcoming environment as the women are gathering before the session begins, consider either lighting one or more candles, providing coffee or other refreshments, or playing worship music, or all of these. (Bring an iPod, smartphone, or tablet and a portable speaker if desired.) Be sure to provide name tags if the women do not know one another or you have new participants in your group. Then, when you are ready to begin, open the group in prayer.

If meeting online, welcome each participant as she joins and encourage the women to talk informally until you are ready to open the group in prayer.

Icebreaker (5 minutes)

Invite the women to share short responses to the following question:

• When was a time you had doubts and needed reassurance about something?

Video (20 minutes)

Play the Week 1 video segment. Invite participants to complete the Video Viewer Guide for Week 1 in the participant workbook as they watch (page 44).

Group Discussion (25–35 minutes, depending on session length)

Note: More material is provided than you will have time to include. Before the session, select what you want to cover.

VIDEO DISCUSSION QUESTIONS

• Amberly focuses on Power, Protection, Process, and Praise as we unpack our memory verse, Psalm 28:7. Which of these speaks most to you and your needs as you look back on the week's reading and reflection?

• How does the portion of the verse, "My heart leaps for joy and with my song, I praise him" make you feel today?

• Have there been times this week when you felt like the psalmist, downcast and uncertain?

• The video this week ends with the Permission Slip, the Permission to Doubt. What does permission to doubt and question mean for you? In what other areas of your spiritual life do you need permission to grow.

PARTICIPANT WORKBOOK DISCUSSION QUESTIONS

1. Our lives are filled with questions. Why is my phone not working? What are we going to have for dinner? Where are my keys? We also ask many questions in our faith journeys. During this study we will normalize asking questions and explore how they can help us to untangle our faith and deepen our intimacy with God as we come to know who God is. Our beginning point is considering that God is a loving Parent who responds to our needs as a loving parent would.

• Why are we sometimes afraid to ask God questions? How can our questions draw us closer to God?

- Read aloud Luke 11:9-13. Think about your parents or loving adults who nurtured and guided you well. What characteristics did they exhibit? Name ways God is a Loving Parent.
- Reflect upon your ordinary day-to-day living. Now think of a time when there was a tragedy or a setback in your life. How did the questions you asked God change as you went from ordinary to extraordinary times?
- After praying the Lord's Prayer this week, how are you able to answer this question: does God care about me and my struggles? Name the ways.

2. We often use the word *good* as our answer to questions. How was your day in school? *Good.* How was your lunch today? *Good.* But God proves Himself to be *truly good* in the witness of Scripture and our own lives. Even through heartache, loss, disappointment, and fear, God proves Himself faithful to us. And if we will recall the faithfulness He has shown us in the past, even when we cannot see it clearly in the present, we will be strengthened and reassured.

- We read several Scripture passages concerning the goodness of God. What other divine characteristics named in scripture did you add to describe God's goodness? (Refer to page 19.)
- When have you answered a question recently with the word *good*? Now say aloud the phrase *God is good.* How does the nuance of the meaning of the word *good* change when we say the phrase *God is good*?
- In Matthew 16:8-12, we discover questions that Jesus asked of his followers—questions that communicated the disciples should not worry about the provision of their needs but should recall the faithfulness of God. Think about all the times we focus on our next need instead of reflecting on the goodness of God. What are some ways we can focus on our past blessings instead of worrying about our next needs?
- Share your responses to the phrase "If I truly understood how good God is and how much He loves me, I would/would not_____." (Refer to page 24.)

3. God is faithful. Many times, we jump to conclusions and worry instead of remembering the faithfulness of God. When we face uncertainties, questions can help us process what we are going through, but only when the questions are grounded in the truth of God and His character can they transition us from panicked questioning to peace.

- How confident are you that God will be with you no matter what? That He will be faithful to take care of all that concerns you? What are your doubts or questions related to God's faithfulness?
- Ask someone to read aloud Matthew 6:25-27. How do these verses reassure us that God is faithful?
- How do you see evidence of the faithfulness of God in your life and in the world? (Refer to page 29.)
- Did you complete the exercise of making a "worry list" and writing beside each worry a statement of God's faithful love and provision (as suggested in "A Practical Next Step" on page 29)? If so, how did this exercise encourage you? How can thanking God for how He is going to meet our needs help to reduce our worry?

4. God is our refuge, especially when things are falling apart. Like a warm blanket covering us in security, God is our refuge in the midst of life's storms and the One who redeems our stories. Even when life doesn't feel safe, we can find security in knowing we are safe in the arms of God.
   - Even though God is our safe place and protector, there are times when a literal refuge is also needed. Where is your safe place? (Refer to page 32.)
   - Reflect on John 14:5-14. Many people dismiss doubting Thomas because of his questions. How can this story encourage us? When was a time you doubted God but later experienced God's protection and hope?
   - What does it mean for you to make God your "safe place"? (Refer to page 34.)
   - Ask someone to read aloud Jeremiah 29:13. Name your feelings after hearing this verse. How does this verse bring you hope and comfort? Discuss what it looks like practically speaking to know, see, believe, and act. (Refer to pages 34–35.)
   - Why is practicing thankfulness for all God has done for us a way to experience refuge? When has thankfulness helped you to remember God's faithfulness and experience God's refuge?

5. God desires to help us see clearly. Our perceptions of God and truth become increasingly clear as we grow in our faith and trust God to heal our spiritual vision. Sometimes healing can be a slow process, yet we can be confident that God is patient and never stops working on our behalf.
   - Read aloud Mark 8:22-26. How are we sometimes like the blind man in this story? What does this story teach us about God? How does it give us hope for our own spiritual blindness?

- Are you trusting God to heal your spiritual blind spots? Do you have the desire to see God more clearly, even if it means letting go of your preconceived notions of Him? Why or why not? (Refer to page 40.)
- Waiting for healing from God is difficult. What are some ways our waiting can be more active than passive?
- The memory verse for week 1 is Psalm 28:7. Ask someone to read aloud this verse. How did God speak to you through this verse this week? How is God inviting you to respond? (Refer to page 43.)

Deeper Conversation (15 minutes)

Divide into smaller groups of two to three for deeper conversation. (Encourage the women to break into different groups each week.) If you'd like, before the session, write on a markerboard or chart paper the questions below. You also could also do this in the form of a handout.

- Where did you see God at work in your life this week?
- Are there areas of your life where trusting God is still an issue? Why?

Closing Prayer (5 minutes)

Close the session by taking personal prayer requests from group members and leading the group in prayer. As you progress to later weeks in the study, you might encourage members to participate in the Closing Prayer by praying out loud for one another and the requests given.

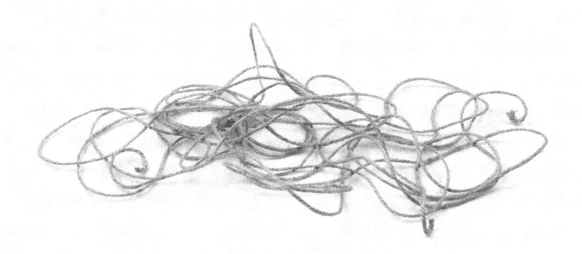

Week 2

How Can I Grow in My Faith?

Leader Notes for the Week

_____

_____

_____

_____

_____

_____

_____

_____

_____

_____

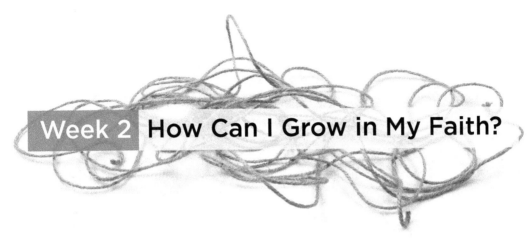

Week 2 How Can I Grow in My Faith?

Leader Prep (Before the Session)

Overview

This week we focused on spiritual growth. God is the one who brings the growth in us, but we can position ourselves for growth and foster growth by cooperating with the work of God in us—and we can mark spiritual growth in our lives. During the week, we looked at five ways we can foster spiritual growth in cooperation with God:

Day 1: Knowing Jesus Personally Grows My Faith

Day 2: The Faith of Others Grows My Faith

Day 3: Remembering God's Faithfulness Grows My Faith

Day 4: Persistent Prayer Grows My Faith

Day 5: Believing Jesus Grows My Faith

Memory Verse

"Truly I tell you, if you have faith as small as a mustard seed, you can say to this mountain, 'Move from here to there,' and it will move. Nothing will be impossible for you."

(Matthew 17:20b)

Daily Questions

Day 1

Jesus's Question: "But what about you?" he asked. "Who do you say I am?" (Matthew 16:15)

The Question We Ask: Who is Jesus to me?

Day 2

Jesus's Question: "Where is your faith?" he asked his disciples. (Luke 8:25)

The Question We Ask: What if my faith wavers?

Day 3

Jesus's Question: "Why does this generation ask for a sign?" (Mark 8:12)

The Question We Ask: How can I have faith when times are hard?

Day 4

Jesus's Question: "However, when the Son of Man comes, will he find faith on the earth?" (Luke 18:8)

The Question We Ask: Why should I keep praying?

Day 5

Jesus's Question: "Don't you believe that I am in the Father, and that the Father is in me?" (John 14:10)

The Question We Ask: Do I really believe Jesus is who He says He is?

What You Will Need

- *Untangling Faith* DVD and DVD player, or equipment to stream the video online
- Bible in two different translations and *Untangling Faith* participant workbook for reference
- container of mustard seeds and a picture of a mustard plant
- markerboard or chart paper and markers (optional)
- stick-on name tags and markers (optional)
- iPod, smartphone, or tablet and portable speaker (optional)

Session Outline

Welcome and Opening Prayer (5–10 minutes, depending on session length)

In order to create a warm, welcoming environment as the women are gathering before the session begins, consider either lighting one or more candles, providing coffee or other refreshments, or playing worship music, or all of these. (Bring an iPod, smartphone, or tablet and a portable speaker if desired.) Be sure to provide name tags if the women do not know one another or you have new participants in your group. Then, when you are ready to begin, open the group in prayer.

If meeting online, welcome each participant as she joins and encourage the women to talk informally until you are ready to open the group in prayer.

Icebreaker (5 minutes)

Invite the women to share short responses to the following question:

- What is something that has helped to shape or strengthen your faith?

Video (20 minutes)

Play the Week 2 video segment. Invite participants to complete the Video Viewer Guide for Week 2 in the participant workbook as they watch (page 77).

Group Discussion (25–35 minutes, depending on session length)

Note: More material is provided than you will have time to include. Before the session, select what you want to cover.

Video Discussion Questions

- Let's read together Matthew 17:20. This week, were there specific mountains to move that you thought about when reading this verse? Did this verse give you confidence or inspiration?
- Could you relate to Amberly's rafting story of having all the right information but not the right outcomes? What does this mean for you? Do you get in your own way?
- As you work to grow in your faith, what does giving yourself permission to fail do for you? How could that change your openness?

Participant Workbook Discussion Questions

1. Knowing Jesus personally grows our faith. Jesus wants to help us know Him. Our faith journey reflects our view of who we believe Jesus is.
   - Read aloud the weekly memory verse, Matthew 17:20b. Allow your group to see and touch the mustard seeds. Now show them a picture of a mustard plant. Our God is such a great gardener! Invite participants to imagine this seed becoming a huge plant, and then their own faith growing into a flourishing plant from the smallest of seeds. Discuss ways we can foster spiritual growth in cooperation with God.
   - Have there been times in your life when God's provision, protection, or power turned your doubts into strengths of your faith? If so, explain briefly. (Refer to page 48.)

- Reflect on the life of Peter. We were reminded he was a contradiction. Describe ways you are sometimes a contradiction like Peter.
- Are you willing to put in the spiritual work to come to know God, trusting that God is seeking you? How can we answer Jesus's question "Who do you say I am?" every day of our lives?
- Share what you believe today about Jesus and why. (Refer to "A Practical Next Step" on page 51.)

2. Faith doesn't have to be perfect to be real, and the faith of others can help grow our faith. In Hebrews 11, we discover many heroes of faith whose lives encourage us on our faith journeys.
   - Ask a couple of group members to read aloud Hebrews 11:1 from two different translations of the Bible. Talk about ways this verse encourages us as we are untangling our faith.
   - Chapter 11 in the Book of Hebrews is filled with faith heroes. Reflect upon your study of that chapter this week. Which of these faith heroes stands out most to you, and why? How are you encouraged by their imperfections, limitations, mistakes, and even spiritual waffling? (Refer to page 56.)
   - In Luke 8:22-25, we encounter a story where the disciples wavered in their faith. Imagine you were in that boat during the storm. How do you think you might have responded to the storm and the question asked by Jesus, "Where is your faith?" When has someone encouraged you to keep the faith when your faith was weak, as Jesus did the disciples? (Refer to page 57.)
   - If you called or visited a friend or mentor this week (as suggested in "A Practical Next Step" on page 57), share about that visit and your conversation.

3. Remembering God's faithfulness helps our faith to grow and develop. We can trust God in the good times and in the not-so-good times when we allow the evidence of God to focus our minds and hearts on Him.
   - Hebrews 11:35-38 acknowledges that people of faith are not excluded from hardships and persecution. What helps you focus on the goodness of God during especially difficult times of life?
   - How does reflecting on the lives of faithful followers of Christ, along with studying the Bible, help us to collect evidence of the goodness and faithfulness of God?
   - What helps you to believe when you do not see? (Refer to page 63.)

- How did creating a time line and reflecting on the ups and downs of your life impact you? (Refer to "A Practical Next Step" on page 64.)

4. Prayer is about building our faith as we wait and come to trust God to answer. Persisting in prayer, while trusting in the character of God, increases our faith.

   - Reliability. Reality. Relationship. Think about the power in these three *R* words. Where do you see God at work in each *R* word in your life? Which is easiest for you and which is most difficult when it comes to trusting God? (Refer to page 67.)

   - Reflect on Luke 18:1-8. Focus on verse 8 and the question asked by Jesus. How would you answer this question if Jesus asked it about you personally?

   - Prayer builds our own faith as we wait and come to trust God to answer. As you wait on God in your prayer life, do you see this activity as active or passive? Explain.

   - After our study this week, are you encouraged to keep on praying? Do you have a plan or format you follow to consistently seek God's face in prayer? If so, share it. (Refer to page 69.)

5. Believing Jesus empowers us to put our faith into action. If we really believe Jesus is who He said He is, it changes our behaviors, thoughts, goals, and entire lives.

   - Why is our faith in Jesus the most precious commodity we can ever possess?

   - Ask someone to read aloud John 14:12. Living out our faith means doing the work of Christ. How does this verse empower you to put your faith into action?

   - Have someone read aloud Psalm 77:11-12. What is the psalmist urging us to do? With the awareness that Jesus is the culminating treasure of all God's works and wonders, what was it like to ponder who Jesus is and what He has done? Share your thoughts from "A Practical Next Step" on page 74.

   - Remember those small mustard seeds and our memory verse, Matthew 17:20b. How did God speak to you through this verse this week? How is God inviting you to respond? (Refer to page 76.)

Deeper Conversation (15 minutes)

Divide into smaller groups of two to three for deeper conversation. (Encourage the women to break into different groups each week.) If you'd like, before the session, write on a markerboard or chart paper the following questions. You could also do this in the form of a handout.

- Where did you see God at work in your life this past week?
- Reflect on that small mustard seed. Now focus on your faith in God. How does an intimate relationship with Jesus allow your faith to grow and grow?

Closing Prayer (5 minutes)

Close the session by taking personal prayer requests from group members and leading the group in prayer. As you progress to later weeks in the study, you might encourage members to participate in the Closing Prayer by praying out loud for one another and the requests given.

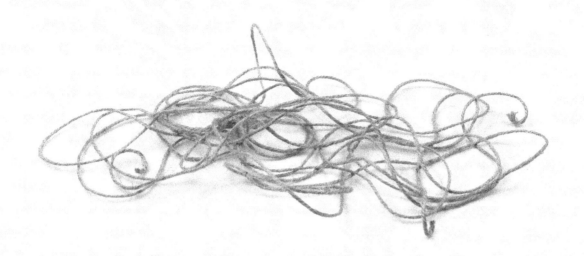

Week 3

Why Should I Pray?

Leader Notes for the Week

_____

_____

_____

_____

_____

_____

_____

_____

_____

_____

Week 3 Why Should I Pray?

Leader Prep (Before the Session)

Overview

Prayer is such a powerful experience. In our week 3 lessons we focused on prayer as a way not to get what we want but to stay in touch with God—with His heart, His voice, His will. This week we explored five facets of prayer:

Day 1: Prayer is Intimate Communication with God

Day 2: Prayer Is Learning to Listen and Look for God

Day 3: Prayer Is Dependent on God's Goodness, Not Mine

Day 4: Prayer Reveals the Desires of My Heart

Day 5: Prayer Enables Me to Choose God's Best

Memory Verse

"This is the confidence we have in approaching God: that if we ask anything according to his will, he hears us."

(1 John 5:14)

Daily Questions

Day 1

Jesus's Question: "What do you want me to do for you?" (Matthew 20:32)

The Question We Ask: Can I trust Jesus with my needs and desires?

Day 2

Jesus's Question: "If I am telling the truth, why don't you believe me?" (John 8:46)

The Question We Ask: Why does it seem God isn't answering my prayer?

Day 3

Jesus's Question: "Do you think that these Galileans were worse sinners than all the other Galileans because they suffered this way?" (Luke 13:2)

The Question We Ask: Does my righteousness (or lack thereof) affect whether or not God answers my prayers?

Day 4

Jesus's Question: "Do you think I cannot call on my Father, and he will at once put at my disposal more than twelve legions of angels? But how then would the Scriptures be fulfilled that say it must happen this way?" (Matthew 26:53-54)

The Question We Ask: Is prayer about more than getting what I want?

Day 5

Jesus's Question: "Did not the Messiah have to suffer these things and then enter his glory?" (Luke 24:26)

The Question We Ask: Am I willing to lay down my agenda for God's?

What You Will Need

- *Untangling Faith* DVD and DVD player, or equipment to stream the video online
- Bible and *Untangling Faith* participant workbook for reference
- markerboard or chart paper and markers (optional)
- stick-on name tags and markers (optional)
- iPod, smartphone, or tablet and portable speaker (optional)

Session Outline

Welcome and Opening Prayer (5–10 minutes, depending on session length)

In order to create a warm, welcoming environment as the women are gathering before the session begins, consider either lighting one or more candles, providing coffee or other refreshments, or playing worship music, or all of these. (Bring an iPod, smartphone, or tablet and a portable speaker if desired.) Be sure to provide name tags if the women do not know one another or you have new participants in your group. Then, when you are ready to begin, open the group in prayer.

If meeting online, welcome each participant as she joins and encourage the women to talk informally until you are ready to open the group in prayer.

Icebreaker (5 minutes)

Invite the women to share short responses to the following question:

- Where is your favorite place to pray?

Video (20 minutes)

Play the Week 3 video segment. Invite participants to complete the Video Viewer Guide for Week 3 in the participant workbook as they watch (page 109).

Group Discussion (25–35 minutes, depending on session length)

Note: More material is provided than you will have time to include. Before the session, select what you want to cover.

VIDEO DISCUSSION QUESTIONS
- As we talk about prayer, how does prayer relate to the freedom to ask?
- Let's read the memory verse, 1 John 5:14, together. What does confidence bring to your prayer life? How about trust?
- How do you see God working in your prayer life this week?
- The Permission Slip this week is Permission to Wonder. How do trust and confidence, community, the caveat, and the covenant work together to allow you this permission in your own prayer life?

PARTICIPANT WORKBOOK DISCUSSION QUESTIONS
1. Prayer is a relationship with God in which you feel safe to communicate what you desire. We long for a safe place in our lives for our uncertainty, and God is that safe place.
   - Read aloud the memory verse, 1 John 5:14. How is this verse often taken out of context or misunderstood?
   - Glance back at the notes you made and share how you answered this question: how do you recognize when God is at work in your life answering prayer? (Refer to page 82.)
   - Think of a great friend. Do you long to talk with her or him? Do you share your troubles, doubts, and joys? Now think about God and your prayer life. Do you take all your troubles, doubts, and joys to God as often and as easily as you share with your closest friends? If not, why do think that is?

- If you used the A.C.T.S. method to help you pray this week (as suggested in "A Practical Next Step" for Day 1), how did it impact your prayer experience?

2. Prayer helps us to hear and see God at work in our lives. As we get to know God in prayer, we become more familiar with His voice and deepen our trust in Him. God longs to share this lifelong adventure of prayer with each one of us.

   - Share your answer to this question: when has God answered your prayers differently from the way you hoped He would, yet, in retrospect, you can see His hand in all of it? (Refer to page 90.)

   - Ask group members to read John 8:42-47. Focus on verse 46b. What would be your response to the question Jesus asked? How has prayer increased your ability to see and hear God? (Refer to page 91.) How has prayer increased your ability to believe what God says?

   - Think of all the times you have been like Mary and not been able to see Jesus. How has prayer opened your eyes to see Jesus? How do you recognize Jesus's activity in your life? (Refer to page 91.)

   - How have you experienced prayer changing you and what you desire? How does prayer help to align your desires with God's desires for you?

3. God does not answer our prayers according to our behavior. What a wonderful feeling it is knowing that God is full of grace, mercy, and compassion.

   - Prayer is powerful not because of our righteousness but because of the righteousness of God. Explain why this statement does or does not resonate with you.

   - Share your responses to these questions: Is it difficult for you to accept that God's answers to your prayers are not determined by your behavior? Why or why not? (Refer to page 96.)

   - Our biblical heroes were not perfect, made mistakes, and used poor judgment from time to time. How does it feel knowing that God's grace and love extend to all his children, and that our imperfections do not disqualify us from being loved, heard, and used by God?

   - When you don't see God answering your prayers, what is your response? (Refer to page 97.)

   - Have any false beliefs been influencing your prayer life? (Refer to "A Practical Next Step" on page 97.)

4. Through prayer and time with God we discover the desires of our hearts and align our desires with God's. God's way is always for our good and the good of the world.

- Read Psalm 37:1-4. Focus on verse 4. What are the desires of your heart, and what does God have to say to you about them? (Refer to "A Practical Next Step" on page 102.)

- How has prayer transformed you? How do you look more like Jesus today than you did five to ten years ago? How do you hope to look more like Jesus five to ten years from now? (Refer to page 101.)

- Ask someone to read aloud Psalm 119:30. What does this verse reveal to you about setting aside your agenda and following God's ways?

- Glance back at "The Question We Ask": Is prayer about more than getting what I want? What are your thoughts in response to this question after this week's lessons?

5. Are we willing to lay down our agendas for God's? Let's face it. Sacrifice is difficult. The bright side is God's agenda is best for us, and sacrificing our agenda for God's allows Him to work powerfully in our lives.

- What are some of the sacrifices you make for yourself and your family? What are some of the sacrifices made by your parents and grandparents for you?

- Jesus chose to follow God's agenda for His life and ours. Compared to the sacrifices Jesus made, why do you think it is so difficult for us to sacrifice our agenda for God's agenda? What is something you are struggling to surrender to God in prayer now? (Refer to page 105.)

- Ask someone to read aloud Romans 8:26. Describe the comfort you feel knowing the Holy Spirit helps us as we pray, interceding for us with "groanings too deep for words" (NASB).

- If someone were to ask you why you pray, how would you respond?

- Return to the week's memory verse, 1 John 5:14. How did God speak to you about this verse this week? How is God inviting you to respond? (Refer to page 108.)

Deeper Conversation (15 minutes)

Divide into smaller groups of two to three for deeper conversation. (Encourage the women to break into different groups each week.) If you'd like, before the session, write on a

markerboard or chart paper the following questions. You could also do this in the form of a handout.

- Where did you see God at work in your life this week?
- How has this focus on prayer encouraged or challenged you?

Closing Prayer (5 minutes)

Close the session by taking personal prayer requests from group members and leading the group in prayer. As you progress to later weeks in the study, you might encourage members to participate in the Closing Prayer by praying out loud for one another and the requests given.

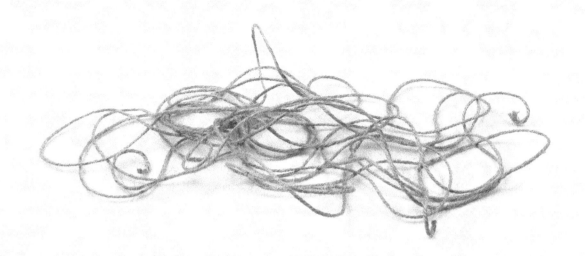

Week 4

What Must I Do to Be Healed?

Leader Notes for the Week

_____

_____

_____

_____

_____

_____

_____

_____

_____

_____

_____

Week 4   What Must I Do to Be Healed?

Leader Prep (Before the Session)

Overview

Consider all the paths we take each day—a path to work, a path to the grocery store, a path to school. This week our lessons reminded us that the path to healing requires our action, dedication, and response, yet only God can bring the healing we need. God is the author of all healing, though sometimes it may not look like what we envision. Healing comes in all shapes and sizes—it can be physical, mental, emotional, or spiritual. While God does not promise physical healing in every instance, God always works to bring healing and wholeness within us, conforming us to the image of Jesus. This week we explored five requirements of the path to healing:

Day 1: The Path to Healing Requires Humility
Day 2: The Path to Healing Requires Seeking Jesus
Day 3: The Path to Healing Requires Understanding
Day 4: The Path to Healing Requires Trusting God's Heart
Day 5: The Path to Healing Requires Surrendering Our Agenda

Memory Verse

> Praise the LORD, my soul,
>   and forget not all his benefits—
> who forgives all your sins
>   and heals all your diseases,
> who redeems your life from the pit
>   and crowns you with love and compassion.
>   (Psalm 103:2-4)

Daily Questions

Day 1

Jesus's Question: Jesus straightened up and asked her, "Woman, where are they? Has no one condemned you?" (John 8:10)

The Question We Ask: Am I worthy of healing?

Day 2

Jesus's Question: "Who touched my clothes?" (Mark 5:30)

The Question We Ask: Can I count on Jesus to heal me?

Day 3

Jesus's Question: "When Jesus looked up and saw a great crowd coming toward him, he said to Philip, 'Where shall we buy bread for these people to eat?'" (John 6:5)

The Question We Ask: Do I understand my deeper needs and Jesus's ability to heal them?

Day 4

Jesus's Question: "Everyone who lives and believes in Me will never die. Do you believe this?" (John 11:25-26 NASB)

The Question We Ask: Can I trust God when healing doesn't come?

Day 5

Jesus's Question: "What is your name?" (Mark 5:9)

The Question We Ask: Does God care about me and my need?

What You Will Need

- *Untangling Faith* DVD and DVD player, or equipment to stream the video online
- Bible and *Untangling Faith* participant workbook for reference
- markerboard or chart paper and markers (optional)
- stick-on name tags and markers (optional)
- iPod, smartphone, or tablet and portable speaker (optional)

Session Outline

Welcome and Opening Prayer (5–10 minutes, depending on session length)

In order to create a warm, welcoming environment as the women are gathering before the session begins, consider either lighting one or more candles, providing coffee or other

refreshments, or playing worship music, or all of these. (Bring an iPod, smartphone, or tablet and a portable speaker if desired.) Be sure to provide name tags if the women do not know one another or you have new participants in your group. Then, when you are ready to begin, open the group in prayer.

If meeting online, welcome each participant as she joins and encourage the women to talk informally until you are ready to open the group in prayer.

Icebreaker (5 minutes)

Invite the women to share short responses to the following question:

- What is a current need for healing in your life or the life of a loved one—whether physical, mental, emotional, or spiritual?

Video (20 minutes)

Play the Week 4 video segment. Invite participants to complete the Video Viewer Guide for Week 4 in the participant workbook as they watch (page 146).

Group Discussion (25–35 minutes, depending on session length)

Note: More material is provided than you will have time to include. Before the session, select what you want to cover.

VIDEO DISCUSSION QUESTIONS

- Our memory verse this week is Psalm 103:2-4 and includes "who forgives all your sins and heals all your diseases." Our question is "What must I do to be healed?" Healing can take on many forms. What are some areas of healing that you thought of this week in your own life?
- Amberly tells a story of a family who asked "have you forgotten who you are?" Have you had a time when you feel you lost a sense of your identity as a child of God. What did this feel like to you?
- One of our words from Amberly is *recall*. Did you make a list this week of the benefits and gifts you have received?
- The Permission Slip this week gives us Permission to Ask. What assurances or confidence do you need to ask God for what you most desire?

PARTICIPANT WORKBOOK DISCUSSION QUESTIONS

1. Our healing is not dependent on our behavior. Jesus desires for all to experience healing and wholeness in Him.
   - Describe the emotions you feel when you consider that, regardless of past or present circumstances, all are eligible for Jesus's healing.
   - Focus on the passage from John 8:2-11. In light of the way Jesus treated the adulterous woman, how are you being invited to view your own struggles? What can we learn from Jesus's example in this story about how to respond to someone who has fallen? (Refer to page 118.)
   - Ask someone to read aloud the memory verse, Psalm 103:2-4. Which phrase or phrases of this passage speak to you?
   - Read silently the passage from 2 Corinthians 12:6-10. How do we see humility in these verses? (Refer to "A Practical Next Step" on page 119.)

2. Healing is not a recipe to follow but a person to seek—Jesus. Even when we do not receive physical healing, we can count on Jesus to respond to our seeking hearts with love and tenderness, granting us the inner peace and freedom we desperately need.
   - Remember the story of Amberly's encounter with the woman at the coffee bar. Have you ever felt like the lonely woman? What was she seeking? How were her prayers answered?
   - Focus on the passage from Mark 5:24b-34. The woman in this passage was a seeker. Describe her experience of waiting on healing and all the ways she sought help. What was she really seeking?
   - Ask someone to read aloud Mark 5:34. When have you needed to hear that reassurance and receive that promise of healing and hope for your life? How do you relate to the woman with the bleeding disorder? (Refer to page 123.)
   - If you employed any of the six *Hs* to seek the Lord for healing, please share your responses. (Refer to page 125.)
   - Was there a time when you sought Jesus for physical healing that did not come? If so, what did God reveal through that situation? What did you learn about yourself, Jesus, and your faith? What did you receive from Jesus instead? (Refer to page 125.)

3. Often we do not have full understanding of our situation or need and what Jesus can do in our lives. But the path to healing requires this kind of understanding.

We must seek to satisfy our deeper needs in Jesus alone. He is our life, and only He can heal our deeper needs.

- From the reading in John 6:1-7 we discover a somewhat familiar Bible story. Why did Jesus really ask Philip the question, "Where shall we buy bread for these people to eat?"
- What are some of our universal soul needs? (Refer to page 131.) Where are some of the places we seek to satisfy those needs? Where should we look to satisfy our deeper needs and find true healing?
- Share your answers to these questions: What are you preoccupied with lately? How does this preoccupation divert your focus from your deeper soul needs to more superficial needs? (Refer to page 130.)
- How is your soul in need of Jesus's healing touch? (Refer to page 131.)

4. We can trust Jesus to redeem our circumstances and bring spiritual healing. Jesus always redeems, restores, and resurrects or brings new life—including spiritual healing wherever it is needed.
   - Death can seem to be the end of the story. But with God, the things we think are over are just the beginning of something new. Share an example of the beginning of something new after a loss.
   - Ask someone to read aloud John 11:26-27. Why is Martha's response so powerful? Do you believe this today? Why or why not? (Refer to page 137.)
   - Turn to the list of miracles on pages 136–137 in your participant workbook. How is the message the common thread in all these miracles, rather than the method or manner?
   - Are you willing to acquiesce to whatever method or manner God has in mind for your healing (or the healing of a loved one)? Explain your response. (Refer to page 137.)

5. The path to healing requires surrendering our agenda. God sees you and your need and wants to set you free from all that holds you captive.
   - What were you like before you met Jesus? How have you changed since then? (Refer to page 142.)
   - Read aloud Mark 5:18-20. Why didn't Jesus let the man who had been demon-possessed get in the boat? What did Jesus want him to do?

- Think of times when your agenda seemed so important. How was God's agenda your true path to healing? What did you have to surrender, and what did that look like or involve? (Refer to page 143.)
- How have you seen the power of God at work in areas where you have been held captive? (Refer to page 143.)
- Return to the week's memory verse, Psalm 103:2-4. How did God speak to you about this verse this week? How is God inviting you to respond? (Refer to page 145.)

Deeper Conversation (15 minutes)

Divide into smaller groups of two to three for deeper conversation. (Encourage the women to break into different groups each week.) If you'd like, before the session, write on a markerboard or chart paper the questions below. You could also do this in the form of a handout.

- Where did you see God at work in your life this week?
- *What must I do to be healed?* Share ways this week's lessons helped you answer this question. What questions still remain?

Closing Prayer (5 minutes)

Close the session by taking personal prayer requests from group members and leading the group in prayer. Encourage members to participate in the Closing Prayer by praying out loud for one another and the requests given.

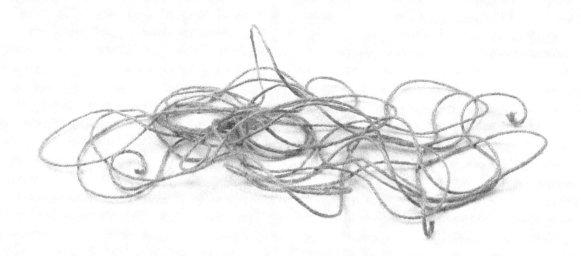

Week 5

What Is God's Plan for Us?

Leader Notes for the Week

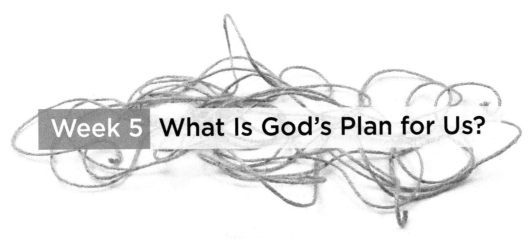

Week 5 What Is God's Plan for Us?

Leader Prep (Before the Session)

Overview

What is God's plan for us? The will of God is something Bible scholars and ordinary people have discussed, studied, discerned, and debated for ages. Rather than dive into the debate, this week we examined some of the irrefutable truths about what God wants for all His people. Knowing some universal truths about God's plans for us can help us to yield our lives—and our wills—to His. In our lessons this week we considered five things we can know with certainty about God's plans for us:

Day 1: God's Plan for Us Is to Have Enduring Faith
Day 2: God's Plan for Us Is to Have a Hope and a Future
Day 3: God's Plan for Us Is Inner Transformation
Day 4: God's Plan for Us Is That We Serve Others
Day 5: God's Plan for Us Is to Live a Life of Love

Memory Verse

Show me your ways, LORD,
  teach me your paths.
Guide me in your truth and teach me,
  for you are God my Savior,
  and my hope is in you all day long.
      (Psalm 25:4-5)

Daily Questions

Day 1

Jesus's Question: "Why did you doubt?" (Matthew 14:26)
The Question We Ask: Where is God when life is hard?

Day 2

Jesus's Question: "Are you not in error because you do not know the Scriptures or the power of God?" (Mark 12:24)

The Question We Ask: Is God going to come through for me?

Day 3

Jesus's Question: "Why do you entertain evil thoughts in your hearts? Which is easier: to say, 'Your sins are forgiven,' or to say, 'Get up and walk'?" (Matthew 9:4-5)

The Question We Ask: If God knows my secret thoughts, is He angry with me?

Day 4

Jesus's Question: "Which of these three do you think was a neighbor to the man who fell into the hands of robbers?" (Luke 10:36)

The Question We Ask: How can I be a good neighbor?

Day 5

Jesus's Question: "Simon son of John, do you love me more than these? . . . Simon son of John, do you love me? . . . Simon son of John, do you love me?" (John 21:15-17)

The Question We Ask: What does loving Jesus look like?

What You Will Need

- *Untangling Faith* DVD and DVD player, or equipment to stream the video online
- Bible and *Untangling Faith* participant workbook for reference
- markerboard or chart paper and markers (optional)
- stick-on name tags and markers (optional)
- iPod, smartphone, or tablet and portable speaker (optional)

Session Outline

Welcome and Opening Prayer (5–10 minutes, depending on session length)

In order to create a warm, welcoming environment as the women are gathering before the session begins, consider either lighting one or more candles, providing coffee or other refreshments, or playing worship music, or all of these. (Bring an iPod, smartphone, or tablet and a portable speaker if desired.) Be sure to provide name tags if the women do not know one another or you have new participants in your group. Then, when you are ready to begin, open the group in prayer.

If meeting online, welcome each participant as she joins and encourage the women to talk informally until you are ready to open the group in prayer.

Icebreaker (5 minutes)

Invite the women to share short responses to the following question:

- What is one question you have about God's plan for your life?

Video (20 minutes)

Play the Week 5 video segment. Invite participants to complete the Video Viewer Guide for Week 5 in the participant workbook as they watch (page 178).

Group Discussion (25–35 minutes, depending on session length)

Note: More material is provided than you will have time to include. Before the session, select what you want to cover.

VIDEO DISCUSSION QUESTIONS
- Our memory verse this week is Psalm 25:4-5. How do the phrases in the verse, "show me," "guide me," and "teach me," connect with you in your daily walk? What are ways you look for God's revelation, guidance, and teaching?
- How can this memory verse become a personal mission statement for us as we look for a stronger faith?
- This week's Permission Slip is Permission to be Uncertain. Even knowing God's unconditional love for us, we all still feel uncertain sometimes in our faith and spiritual life. Where do you see God's assurances for you when you do feel uncertain?

PARTICIPANT WORKBOOK DISCUSSION QUESTIONS
1. God's plan for us is to have enduring faith. Though God doesn't cause challenges to teach us lessons, He does redeem them for our good and our growth. God strengthens our faith through the storms of life.
   - In the story of Jesus walking on the water found in Matthew 14:22-33, Jesus asked Peter why he doubted Him. Why do we doubt God during the storms in our lives? When was a time when you doubted and Jesus reached out for you?
   - Ask someone to read aloud the memory verse, Psalm 25:4-5. How does this verse help us to have an enduring faith in God? According to this verse, what is God's part and what is our part?

- When you struggle to trust God, what motivates you to keep on going? How does recalling the good God has done in the past help you? How often do you take the time to recall the works of God? (Refer to page 151.)
- If you were one of the apostles, which of Jesus's miraculous acts would seem most remarkable to you? Why? (Refer to page 151.)
- Did you connect with someone this week whose faith has endured and grown through difficult times? If so, share what you learned from this person. (Refer to "A Practical Next Step" on page 152.)

2. God's plan for us is to have a hope and a future. Because of God's promises, passion, and power, we can be confident God is working for our good.
   - Ask someone to read aloud Jeremiah 29:11. How does Jeremiah 29:4-10 give us a fuller understanding of this verse? Knowing this, how can Jeremiah 29:11 comfort us in our difficult situations today?
   - How do the words of Jeremiah 29:11 pertain to Jesus and His followers in light of the cross?
   - Reflect on Mark 12:18-24. The Sadducees asked Jesus a trick question in verse 23. What was the motivation behind their question? How did Jesus respond, and what was the intent of His question?
   - What makes it difficult for you to place your confidence in God's promises (His Word), God's passion (His heart), and God's power (His deeds in the Bible and our own lives)? Which of these three *P*s is most challenging for you to trust, and why? (Refer to page 159.)

3. God's plan for us is inner transformation. God knows our hearts and calls us in love toward healing and wholeness—toward His best for us—which includes not only our outward obedience but also our inner messaging. God's desire is that we would walk in freedom on the inside and outside.
   - What does the term "God's will" mean to you?
   - Read aloud Matthew 9:1-8. What does it mean to "entertain" evil or negative thoughts? Practically speaking, how can you "take captive every thought" (2 Corinthians 10:5)? (Refer to page 165.)
   - Why do you think Jesus prioritizes the inner life over the outer one? (Refer to page 166.)

- Ask someone to read aloud Psalm 139:23-24. How is God offering you grace and calling you toward a heart change? (Refer to "A Practical Next Step" on page 166.)

4. God's plan for us is that we serve others. Because God loves us, we can serve others in love and be a good neighbor. Being a neighbor following the example of Christ is not self-deprecation but humble servanthood made possible because of our confidence in our identity in Him and His unconditional love for us.

   - Reflect on the passage from Luke 10:25-37. What do you know about the historical background of the relationship between the Jews and the Samaritans? Why is this context important to understand this parable? (Refer to page 169.)
   - How does Jesus define being a good neighbor in the parable? How did Jesus show neighboring in His life? (Refer to page 170.)
   - Before we can practice real "neighboring" with a servant's heart, what must we receive from God? Why is this necessary? What is keeping you from letting God love you? (Refer to "A Practical Next Step" on page 171.)
   - Share some ways you can practice being a good neighbor to others.

5. God's plan for us is to live a life of love. When we choose to follow Jesus, we are choosing a life of love and service. And this is possible only because we love Jesus. Loving Jesus means loving others.

   - Read aloud John 21:15-19. Why did Jesus ask Peter the same question three times?
   - What are some ways we can feed Jesus's sheep? What ideas did you add to the list in Day 5? (Refer to page 175.)
   - How would you explain what it means to live a life of love? What does loving Jesus look like in your life? How would an observer of your life know that you follow and love Jesus? (Refer to page 175.)
   - Read the memory verse, Psalm 25:4-5, once more. What word or phrase catches your attention and speaks to you? How is God inviting you to respond? (Refer to page 177.)

Deeper Conversation (15 minutes)

Divide into smaller groups of two to three for deeper conversation. (Encourage the women to break into different groups each week.) If you'd like, before the session, write on a markerboard or chart paper the questions below. You could also do this in the form of a handout.

- Where did you see God at work in your life this week?
- How would you explain God's plans for us after studying this week's passages through the eyes of Jesus?

Closing Prayer (5 minutes)

Close the session by taking personal prayer requests from group members and leading the group in prayer. Encourage members to participate in the Closing Prayer by praying out loud for one another and the requests given.

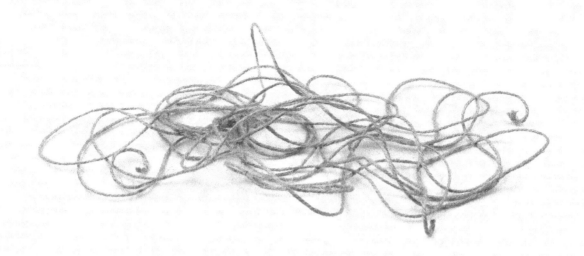

Week 6

What Does It Mean to Follow God?

Leader Notes for the Week

_____

_____

_____

_____

_____

_____

_____

_____

_____

_____

_____

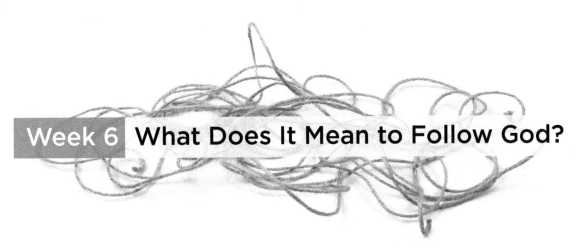

Week 6 What Does It Mean to Follow God?

Leader Prep (Before the Session)

Overview

We are known to be God's followers by the way we live our lives. Following God means examining the things Jesus said and did—the way He served, the lives He touched, the love He showed, and the questions He asked—and then living as He lived. When we live like Jesus, we fulfill the call of Micah 6:8—to act justly, love mercy, and walk humbly with our God. This week we explored five ways we can follow God in the footsteps of Jesus:

Day 1: Following God Means Offering Compassion Instead of Judgment
Day 2: Following God Means Practicing Empathy
Day 3: Following God Means Being Humble
Day 4: Following God Means Being Born of the Spirit
Day 5: Following God Means Taking Up Your Cross

Memory Verse

He has shown you, O mortal, what is good. And what does the LORD require of you? To act justly and to love mercy and to walk humbly with your God.

(Micah 6:8)

Daily Questions

Day 1

Jesus's Question: "Why do you see the splinter that's in your brother's or sister's eye, but don't notice the log in your own eye? How can you say to your brother or sister, 'Let me take the splinter out of your eye,' when there's a log in your own eye?" (Matthew 7:3-4 CEB)

The Question We Ask: What does Jesus say about judging others?

Day 2

Jesus's Question: "Do you see this woman?" (Luke 7:44)

The Question We Ask: How can I see others as Jesus sees them?

Day 3

Jesus's Question: "What were you arguing about on the road?" (Mark 9:33)

The Question We Ask: What does humility look like?

Day 4

Jesus's Question: "If I have told you about earthly things and you don't believe, how will you believe if I tell you about heavenly things?" (John 3:10)

The Question We Ask: How can I have eternal life?

Day 5

Jesus's Question: "What good will it be for someone to gain the whole world, yet forfeit their soul?" (Matthew 16:26)

The Question We Ask: What do I have to give up for Jesus?

What You Will Need

- *Untangling Faith* DVD and DVD player, or equipment to stream the video online
- Bible and *Untangling Faith* participant workbook for reference
- markerboard or chart paper and markers (optional)
- stick-on name tags and markers (optional)
- iPod, smartphone, or tablet and portable speaker (optional)

Session Outline

Welcome and Opening Prayer (5–10 minutes, depending on session length)

In order to create a warm, welcoming environment as the women are gathering before the session begins, consider either lighting one or more candles, providing coffee or other refreshments, or playing worship music, or all of these. (Bring an iPod, smartphone, or tablet and a portable speaker if desired.) Be sure to provide name tags if the women do not know one another or you have new participants in your group. Then, when you are ready to begin, open the group in prayer.

If meeting online, welcome each participant as she joins and encourage the women to talk informally until you are ready to open the group in prayer.

Icebreaker (5 minutes)

Invite the women to share short responses to the following question:

- Who has been a role model for you of what it means to follow Jesus?

Video (20 minutes)

Play the Week 6 video segment. Invite participants to complete the Video Viewer Guide for Week 6 in the participant workbook as they watch (page 215).

Group Discussion (25–35 minutes, depending on session length)

Note: More material is provided than you will have time to include. Before the session, select what you want to cover.

VIDEO DISCUSSION QUESTIONS

- Do you feel any clearer about what it means to follow God after our six-week journey? What stands out to you from your experiences?
- Read Micah 6:8 aloud together. Amberly parsed the verse into "Past," "Position," and "Pondering." How do these three together—our past, our identity or position, and then our constant questioning and pondering—work for a stronger faith?

PARTICIPANT WORKBOOK DISCUSSION QUESTIONS

1. Following God means offering compassion instead of judgment. God calls us to love others in the same way that He loves us. Three *Rs* can help us steer clear of judgment and embrace compassion: relationship, reality, and restraint.
   - Ask members to share examples of ways to put this verse into action.
   - Read aloud Matthew 7:1-5 from the Sermon on the Mount, in which Jesus addresses our tendency to judge others. Why does judging others come so naturally to us? What does God desire of us instead?
   - How can the three *R* parameters help us avoid judging others?
   - When or for what reasons do you find yourself judging others? How has judging others affected your relationships? (Refer to pages 185–186.)
   - What are some practical ways we can offer compassion instead of judging others? Is there an example from your own life you might share?
2. Following God means practicing empathy. God calls us to empathize rather than judge because empathy helps us to love others as we are loved by God.

- Reflect on Luke 7:36-47. How did Jesus demonstrate empathy in this story?
- Imagine you are the woman who anointed Jesus's feet. Describe the emotions you might be experiencing.
- When have you felt unseen? Undervalued? (Refer to page 190.) As a result of that experience, were you empowered to show empathy to others? Why or why not?
- How does it make you feel to realize that Jesus saw this woman, despite her past failures? (Refer to page 191.) How does it feel to know that Jesus sees you through eyes of love and grace?

3. Following God means being humble. Humility is the key to true greatness. Jesus asked his disciples to take their eyes from themselves and focus on Kingdom work—to serve and love others with humility.
   - Why do you think humility is a vital component of being a follower of Jesus?
   - Reflect on the conversation in Mark 9:33-35. How do we see a lack of humility in some of the disciples? What was Jesus's response, and how did he demonstrate humility as he offered it?
   - In your own words, define "greatness" and "humility" in view of Jesus's question to the disciples. (Refer to page 199.)
   - How did Jesus model being least of all? How does His example inspire you to be more like Him?
   - Think of the humblest person you know. What qualities does he or she possess? How might you increase those qualities in your life?

4. Following God means being born of the Spirit. Like Nicodemus, we can struggle to understand what that means. Through His sacrifice on the cross, Jesus takes us from death to life. We find new life in Jesus by being spiritually reborn through faith in Him.
   - Turn to John 3:2-15. Why did Nicodemus go to Jesus? Why did he have a hard time understanding Jesus's words about being born again? How did Jesus explain it?
   - Ask someone to read aloud John 3:16. Imagine you are meeting someone who has never heard this verse. How would you describe the meaning of being born again?
   - Read aloud Luke 9:23. What does it mean to deny ourselves, take up our cross daily, and follow Jesus?
   - This week you have had time to ponder this question: what are you most excited about when it comes to following Jesus? Share your responses with the group. (Refer to page 207.)

5. Following God means taking up your cross, which is giving up your own plans and agenda for your life. What God promises in return is not just rewards in heaven but eternal, abundant life that begins here and now and continues forever. The rewards of following Jesus far outweigh the costs. What a joy it is knowing that Jesus is always with us no matter what!

   - Read aloud this statement: the rewards of following Jesus far outweigh the costs. What does that mean to you? How have you experienced this to be true in your own life?

   - Reflect on Matthew 16:24-27. What are the costs and rewards of following Jesus? For you, what is the most daunting cost of following Jesus, and why? For you, what is the greatest reward of following Jesus, and why? (Refer to the chart and questions on pages 211–212.)

   - Have you written a personal mission statement for following Jesus—or would you like to (see "A Practical Next Step" on page 212)? If Jesus calls all of us to follow Him by living as He did (offering compassion, practicing empathy, being humble, and so forth), why is it helpful to write a personal mission statement for following Him?

   - Read aloud this week's memory verse, Micah 6:8. How is God speaking to you through this verse and inviting you to respond? (Refer to page 214.)

Deeper Conversation (15 minutes)

Divide into smaller groups of two to three for deeper conversation. (Encourage the women to break into different groups each week.) If you'd like, before the session, write on a markerboard or chart paper the questions below. You could also do this in the form of a handout.

- Where did you see God at work in your life this week?
- How have this week's lessons further equipped or inspired you to follow God?

Closing Prayer (5 minutes)

Close the session by taking personal prayer requests from group members and leading the group in prayer. Encourage members to participate in the Closing Prayer by praying out loud for one another and the requests given.

Video Viewer Guide Answers

Week 1

strength

shield

helps

trusts

joy

praise

doubts

Week 2

tell

mustard seed

will move

Nothing

get it right

Week 3

confidence / approaching

his will

hears

wonder

Week 4

Praise

Worship

forget not

forgives

heals

redeems

crowns

ask

Week 5

Show

Guide / teach

hope

uncertain

Week 6

good

mortal

require of you

Act

Adore

Accompany

need reminders

Watch videos based on *Untangling Faith: Reclaiming Hope in the Questions Jesus Asked* with Amberly Neese through Amplify Media.

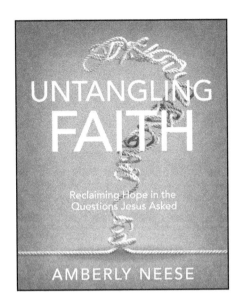

Amplify Media is a multimedia platform that delivers high-quality, searchable content with an emphasis on Wesleyan perspectives for churchwide, group, or individual use on any device at any time. In a world of sometimes overwhelming choices, Amplify gives church leaders and congregants media capabilities that are contemporary, relevant, effective, and, most important, affordable and sustainable.

With *Amplify Media* church leaders can:

- Provide a reliable source of Christian content through a Wesleyan lens for teaching, training, and inspiration in a customizable library
- Deliver their own preaching and worship content in a way the congregation knows and appreciates
- Build the church's capacity to innovate with engaging content and accessible technology
- Equip the congregation to better understand the Bible and its application
- Deepen discipleship beyond the church walls

Ask your group leader or pastor about Amplify Media
and sign up today at www.AmplifyMedia.com.

CPSIA information can be obtained
at www.ICGtesting.com
Printed in the USA
LVHW050146250223
740095LV00002B/4

9 781791 028763